MW01679478

TAKE THE TRIP

The whens and wheres of travel

"The world is a book and those who do not travel read only one page."

— **AUGUSTINE OF HIPPO**

The compass icon indicates pages that are interactive. Scratch, check off, or jot down a memory. But really, every page is yours to write, highlight, and make your own!

INTRO

USA

THE WORLD

THEMED TRAVEL

TOOLKIT

MEMORY LOGS

WELCOME TO YOUR JOURNEY

There are places in this world that change you. Some do it quietly: a sunrise over a city you've never seen, the first breath of air somewhere far from home. Others arrive louder: a winding road, a crowded market, a table full of strangers who somehow feel familiar by dessert.

Travel isn't only about where you go. It's about when you go: the season, the moment in your life, the version of you who steps onto the plane and the one who returns. Each journey adds a layer. Each horizon stretches a little wider.

Great explorers and storytellers like Anthony Bourdain reminded us that the world is meant to be tasted, wandered, and shared. Others who once roamed freely now live on through their words and memories, a gentle reminder that our time to explore is precious and finite. The privilege of being here—of having the chance to see more, feel more, and understand more—is not something to postpone.

This book is an invitation. Not a checklist to rush through, but a companion for dreaming, planning, and savoring the act of discovery. It's a place to map your curiosities, celebrate your adventures, and imagine the ones still waiting.

Go somewhere in every season. Chase warmth. Wander into the cold. Follow color, light, and curiosity wherever they lead. The world is vast, generous, and endlessly surprising.

And the best part?
You're just getting started.

HOW TO NAVIGATE YOUR TRAVEL STORY

GO WITH WONDER AND START TO WANDER!

THINK OF THIS BOOK AS A LAUNCHPAD, NOT A RULEBOOK. There's no right way to use it. Only your way. Flip around. Skip ahead. Dog-ear pages. Scratch off places you've been and circle the ones calling your name. Rip a page out if you want to. Let it be equal parts dreaming and doing.

IF YOU'RE USING IT SOLO, treat it like a personal adventure lab. Wander through the pages, challenge yourself to imagine new places, and give your future trips something to aim for. For couples, it becomes a shared wish list and a fun way to say, "Where next?"

FAMILIES CAN TURN IT INTO A GROUP PROJECT, letting everyone vote on destinations and building excitement long before the bags are packed. And with friends? It's fuel for big ideas, spontaneous plans, and the kind of trips you'll laugh about for years.

As you mark the places you want to go, remember that travel isn't just a someday fantasy... it's something you can plan toward. A little intention, a little saving, and a lot of curiosity go a long way. Every marked destination is a promise to your future self.

A DOSE OF REALITY: Travel costs money. (We checked. Unfortunately, airlines still prefer payment over good vibes). The good news is that this book isn't just about dreaming. It also helps you turn those dreams into plans. Inside, you'll find simple strategies and smarter ways to save and budget for your adventures. Approaches that feel a lot more motivating than dropping spare coins into a dusty piggy bank. Think of it as building a travel fund with intention, creativity, and a clear destination in mind.

MOST IMPORTANTLY, HAVE FUN WITH IT. The world is wide, surprising, and closer than it seems. Start anywhere. Chase what excites you. And let this book be the spark that turns "we should go sometime" into "we're going."

WHICH SEASON CALLS YOU TO EXPLORE?

01 Your ideal morning in a new place starts with:

A. Sunshine, open air, and a plan to stay outside all day

B. Crisp air and a long scenic walk with changing colors

C. A cozy café and a slow, quiet start

D. Fresh blooms, light layers, and wandering with no schedule

02 You choose destinations based on:

A. Beaches, festivals, and lively energy

B. Landscapes, culture, and seasonal beauty

C. Comfort, contrast, or an escape from extremes

D. Renewal, nature, and the feeling of a fresh start

03 Your perfect travel photo captures:

A. Bright skies and movement

B. Texture, color, and atmosphere

C. Intimate moments and quiet scenes

D. Growth, water, or something coming to life

04 When packing, you prioritize:

A. Freedom to move and stay active

B. Versatility for changing weather

C. Comfort and warmth

D. Lightness and simplicity

05 The pace of your ideal trip is:

A. Energetic and social

B. Balanced and immersive

C. Slow and restorative

D. Curious and spontaneous

Calculate which option A, B, C, or D you selected most. Your most frequent answer reveals your travel personality below.

QUIZ RESULTS

MOSTLY A's: SUMMER SEEKER

You travel for energy, connection, and full days under open skies. You're drawn to places that buzz with life and warmth. Exploration, for you, is about celebration of people, culture, and the joy of being fully present in the moment.

MOSTLY B's: FALL WANDERER

You are thoughtful and observant, happiest when surrounded by beauty and meaning. You savor transitions in landscapes and in life. Travel is your way of deepening perspective and collecting stories that stay with you.

MOSTLY C's: WINTER ESCAPIST

You seek contrast and restoration. Whether chasing snow or sun, your journeys are intentional pauses that recharge you. You understand that travel can be both adventure and refuge.

MOSTLY D's: SPRING BLOOMER

You are guided by curiosity and renewal. You travel to feel inspired, to grow, and to welcome change. Every trip is a beginning... a chance to see the world, and yourself, with fresh eyes.

FROM SEA TO SHINING SEA

Alaska is often a bucket-list destination, but its distance and cost keep total visitor numbers relatively low.

ADVENTURE ARCHIVE

Scratch off the states you've visited with a coin.

Visiting all 50 states is relatively rare. The average American has visited about 16–17 states. **Fewer than 2%** have visited all 50 states. **How many have you visited?**

LEAST-VISITED U.S. STATES

01 **ALASKA** ~13% of Americans have visited
02 **NORTH DAKOTA** ~15%
03 **IDAHO** ~19%
04 **MONTANA** ~19%
05 **NEBRASKA** ~19%

MOST-VISITED U.S. STATES

01 **FLORIDA** ~61–64% of Americans have visited
02 **NEW YORK** ~55–56%
03 **CALIFORNIA** ~50–54%
04 **TEXAS** ~51–52%
05 **PENNSYLVANIA** ~48%

WHICH STATE(S) ARE ON YOUR BUCKET LIST?

☐ ______________________

☐ ______________________

OPTIMAL SEASON KEY

SPRING = MARCH, APRIL, MAY

SUMMER = JUNE, JULY, AUGUST

AUTUMN = SEPTEMBER, OCTOBER, NOVEMBER

WINTER = DECEMBER, JANUARY, FEBRUARY

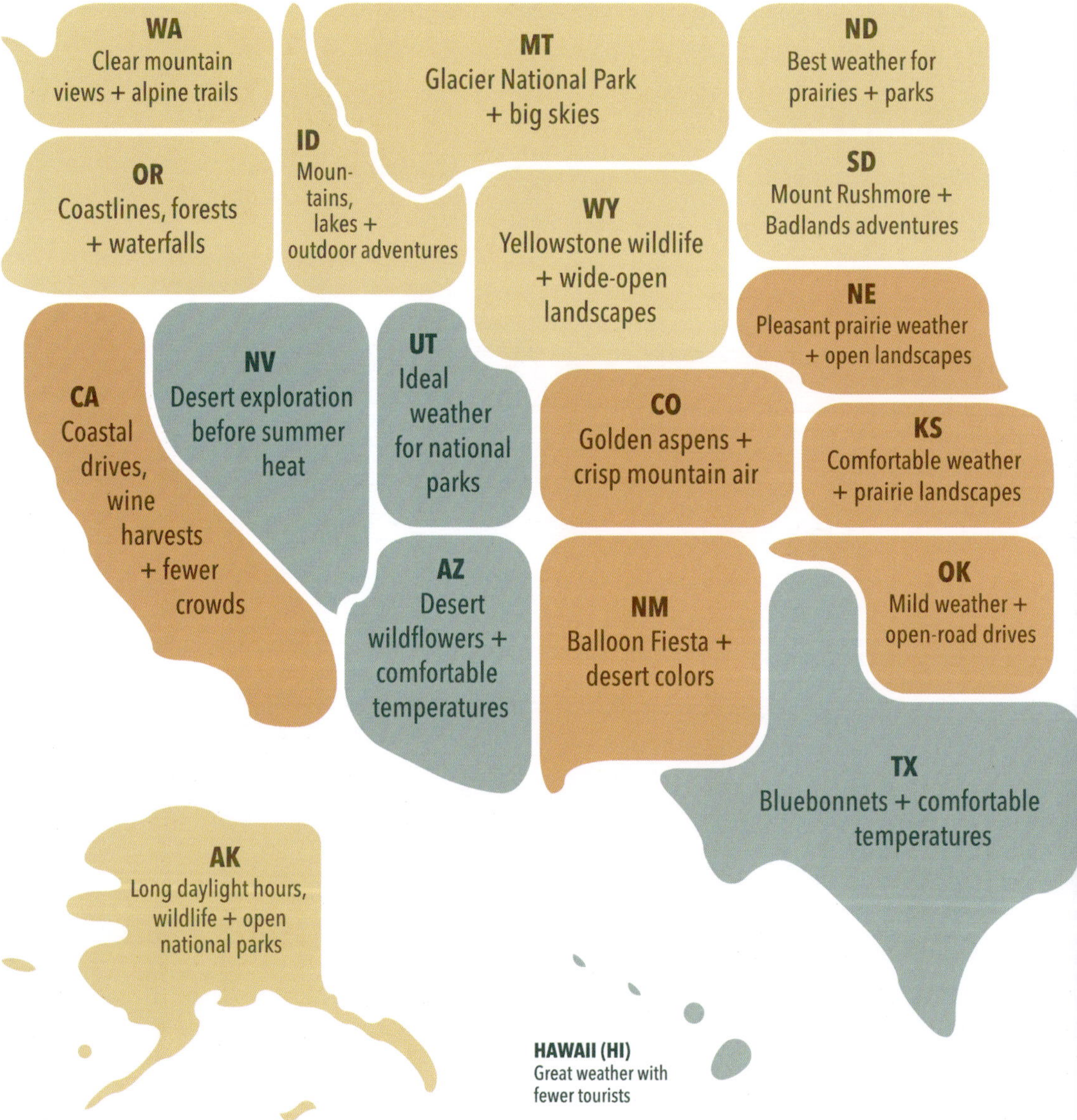

AMERICA AT ITS MOST BEAUTIFUL

THE ULTIMATE SEASONAL GUIDE TO THE 50 STATES

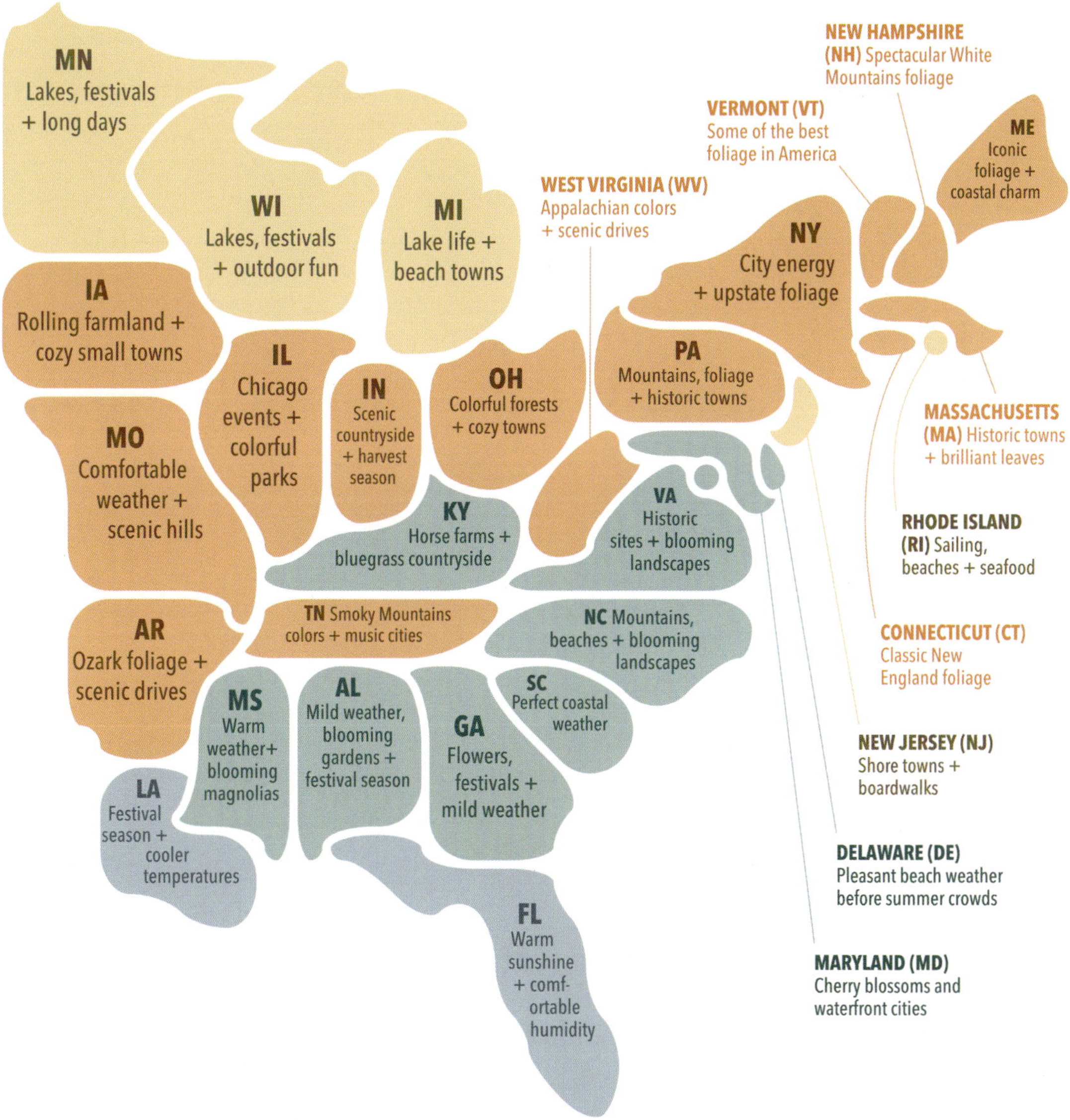

DISCOVER AMERICA, ONE STATE AT A TIME

From iconic landmarks to hidden gems, every U.S. state has its own story, flavor, and adventure waiting to be discovered. This guide highlights the best time to visit, top attractions, local treasures, must-try food, festivals, natural wonders, and handy travel tips. Whether you're planning a road trip, weekend getaway, or lifelong bucket-list journey, these pages will help you make every visit unforgettable.

SNAPSHOTS OF THE 50 UNITED STATES

Little River Canyon, AL

ALABAMA

YELLOWHAMMER STATE

BEST TIME TO VISIT	March–May
POPULAR ATTRACTIONS	Gulf Shores • U.S. Space & Rocket Center • Birmingham Civil Rights Institute
HIDDEN GEMS	Dauphin Island • Little River Canyon National Preserve • Fairhope
MUST EAT	Fried Green Tomatoes
#1 FESTIVAL	Hangout Music Festival
TOP NATURAL WONDER	Little River Canyon
TRAVEL TIP	Skip the summer humidity.

ALASKA

THE LAST FRONTIER

BEST TIME TO VISIT	June–August
POPULAR ATTRACTIONS	Denali National Park · Glacier Bay National Park · Northern Lights
HIDDEN GEMS	Talkeetna · Kenai Fjords National Park · Kodiak
MUST EAT	King Crab
#1 FESTIVAL	Iditarod
TOP NATURAL WONDER	Denali
TRAVEL TIP	Everything is bigger, including the distances.

Denali, the highest mountain peak in North America

Grand Canyon, AZ

ARIZONA

GRAND CANYON STATE

BEST TIME TO VISIT October–April

POPULAR ATTRACTIONS Grand Canyon • Sedona • Antelope Canyon

HIDDEN GEMS Bisbee • Petrified Forest National Park • Horseshoe Bend

MUST EAT Sonoran Hot Dog

#1 FESTIVAL Tucson Gem Show

TOP NATURAL WONDER Grand Canyon

TRAVEL TIP Avoid July unless you enjoy oven settings.

ARKANSAS

THE NATURAL STATE

BEST TIME TO VISIT April–June

POPULAR ATTRACTIONS Hot Springs • Ozark Mountains • Crystal Bridges Museum of American Art

HIDDEN GEMS Buffalo National River • Eureka Springs • Mount Magazine

MUST EAT Fried Catfish

#1 FESTIVAL Bikes, Blues & BBQ

TOP NATURAL WONDER Buffalo National River

TRAVEL TIP The backroads are the best roads.

Buffalo National River, AR

Yosemite's "Firefall" illusion (two weeks in mid-to-late February)

CALIFORNIA

THE GOLDEN STATE

BEST TIME TO VISIT April–June, September–October

POPULAR ATTRACTIONS Yosemite National Park · Golden Gate Bridge · Disneyland Park

HIDDEN GEMS Lassen Volcanic National Park · Carmel-by-the-Sea · Anza-Borrego Desert State Park

MUST EAT Fish Tacos

#1 FESTIVAL Coachella

TOP NATURAL WONDER Yosemite Valley

TRAVEL TIP Pick a region — it's basically a country.

COLORADO

THE CENTENNIAL STATE

BEST TIME TO VISIT	June–Sept (hiking) / Jan–March (skiing)
POPULAR ATTRACTIONS	Rocky Mountain National Park · Aspen · Garden of the Gods
HIDDEN GEMS	Great Sand Dunes National Park · Ouray · Telluride
MUST EAT	Green Chili
#1 FESTIVAL	Telluride Bluegrass Festival
TOP NATURAL WONDER	Maroon Bells
TRAVEL TIP	Hydrate. Altitude is real.

Maroon Bells in Colorado during fall season

Kent Falls State Park, CT

CONNECTICUT

THE CONSTITUTION STATE

BEST TIME TO VISIT	September–October
POPULAR ATTRACTIONS	Mystic · Yale University · Gillette Castle State Park
HIDDEN GEMS	Essex · Kent Falls State Park · Thimble Islands
MUST EAT	Lobster Roll
#1 FESTIVAL	Durham Fair
TOP NATURAL WONDER	Kent Falls
TRAVEL TIP	Fall foliage here is elite.

DELAWARE

THE FIRST STATE

BEST TIME TO VISIT May–September

POPULAR ATTRACTIONS Rehoboth Beach • Dover • Nemours Estate

HIDDEN GEMS Cape Henlopen State Park • Lewes • Bombay Hook National Wildlife Refuge

MUST EAT Blue Crab

#1 FESTIVAL Firefly Music Festival

TOP NATURAL WONDER Cape Henlopen

TRAVEL TIP Small state. Big beach charm.

World War II Observation Tower at Cape Henlopen State Park, DE

Everglades National Park, FL

FLORIDA

THE SUNSHINE STATE

BEST TIME TO VISIT	November–April
POPULAR ATTRACTIONS	Walt Disney World • Miami Beach • Everglades National Park
HIDDEN GEMS	Dry Tortugas National Park • St. Augustine • Anna Maria Island
MUST EAT	Key Lime Pie
#1 FESTIVAL	Gasparilla
TOP NATURAL WONDER	Everglades
TRAVEL TIP	Summer = daily 3pm thunderstorms.

GEORGIA

PEACH STATE

BEST TIME TO VISIT	March–May
POPULAR ATTRACTIONS	Savannah • Atlanta • Blue Ridge Mountains
HIDDEN GEMS	Dahlonega • Tallulah Gorge State Park • Jekyll Island
MUST EAT	Peach Cobbler
#1 FESTIVAL	Masters Tournament
TOP NATURAL WONDER	Tallulah Gorge
TRAVEL TIP	Spring is perfection.

Tallulah Gorge, GA

Nā Pali Coast in Kauai, HI

HAWAII

ALOHA STATE

BEST TIME TO VISIT	April–June, September–October
POPULAR ATTRACTIONS	Waikiki Beach • Hawaii Volcanoes National Park • Road to Hana
HIDDEN GEMS	Nā Pali Coast • Lanai City • Pololu Valley
MUST EAT	Poke
#1 FESTIVAL	Merrie Monarch Festival
TOP NATURAL WONDER	Nā Pali Coast
TRAVEL TIP	Island hop if you can.

IDAHO

GEM STATE

BEST TIME TO VISIT June–September

POPULAR ATTRACTIONS Boise • Sun Valley Resort • Shoshone Falls

HIDDEN GEMS Sawtooth Mountains • McCall • Craters of the Moon National Monument

MUST EAT Finger Steaks

#1 FESTIVAL Western Idaho Fair

TOP NATURAL WONDER Sawtooth Mountains

TRAVEL TIP Way more than potatoes.

Sawtooth Mountains, ID

French Canyon, Starved Rock State Park, IL

ILLINOIS

PRAIRIE STATE

BEST TIME TO VISIT	May–October
POPULAR ATTRACTIONS	Chicago · Millennium Park · Navy Pier
HIDDEN GEMS	Galena · Starved Rock State Park · Springfield
MUST EAT	Deep Dish Pizza
#1 FESTIVAL	Lollapalooza
TOP NATURAL WONDER	Starved Rock
TRAVEL TIP	Winters are not for the faint of heart.

INDIANA

HOOSIER STATE

BEST TIME TO VISIT May–October

POPULAR ATTRACTIONS Indianapolis · Indianapolis Motor Speedway · Indiana Dunes National Park

HIDDEN GEMS Nashville · Turkey Run State Park · Madison

MUST EAT Pork Tenderloin Sandwich

#1 FESTIVAL Indy 500

TOP NATURAL WONDER Indiana Dunes

TRAVEL TIP Lake Michigan sunsets surprise people.

Beach on Lake Michigan in Indiana Dunes National Park

Maquoketa Caves State Park, IA

IOWA

HAWKEYE STATE

BEST TIME TO VISIT May–October

POPULAR ATTRACTIONS Des Moines · Field of Dreams Movie Site · Amana Colonies

HIDDEN GEMS Decorah · Maquoketa Caves State Park · High Trestle Trail Bridge

MUST EAT Sweet Corn

#1 FESTIVAL Iowa State Fair

TOP NATURAL WONDER Maquoketa Caves

TRAVEL TIP Yes, the fair is worth it.

KANSAS

SUNFLOWER STATE

BEST TIME TO VISIT	May–June, September–October
POPULAR ATTRACTIONS	Wichita • Topeka • Monument Rocks
HIDDEN GEMS	Tallgrass Prairie National Preserve • Lindsborg • Strataca
MUST EAT	BBQ Brisket
#1 FESTIVAL	Kansas State Fair
TOP NATURAL WONDER	Monument Rocks
TRAVEL TIP	The sunsets steal the show.

Monument Rocks, KS

Mammoth Cave National Park, KY

KENTUCKY

BLUEGRASS STATE

BEST TIME TO VISIT April–June

POPULAR ATTRACTIONS Louisville • w
• Mammoth Cave National Park

HIDDEN GEMS Bardstown • Red River Gorge • Paducah

MUST EAT Hot Brown

#1 FESTIVAL Kentucky Derby

TOP NATURAL WONDER Mammoth Cave

TRAVEL TIP Bourbon trails are a thing. A delicious thing.

LOUISIANA

PELICAN STATE

BEST TIME TO VISIT	February–May
POPULAR ATTRACTIONS	New Orleans • French Quarter • Audubon Zoo
HIDDEN GEMS	Avery Island • Oak Alley Plantation • Natchitoches
MUST EAT	Gumbo
#1 FESTIVAL	Mardi Gras
TOP NATURAL WONDER	Atchafalaya Basin
TRAVEL TIP	Beware the humidity. Embrace the jazz.

Atchafalaya Basin, LA

Jordan Pond in Acadia National Park, ME

MAINE

PINE TREE STATE

BEST TIME TO VISIT June–September

POPULAR ATTRACTIONS Portland · Acadia National Park · Bar Harbor

HIDDEN GEMS Camden Hills State Park · Rockland · Schoodic Peninsula

MUST EAT Lobster Roll

#1 FESTIVAL Maine Lobster Festival

TOP NATURAL WONDER Acadia National Park

TRAVEL TIP Sunrise at Cadillac Mountain = must-do.

MARYLAND

OLD LINE STATE

BEST TIME TO VISIT	May–October
POPULAR ATTRACTIONS	Baltimore · National Aquarium · Annapolis Historic District
HIDDEN GEMS	Assateague Island · Ellicott City · Catoctin Mountain Park
MUST EAT	Crab Cakes
#1 FESTIVAL	Preakness Stakes
TOP NATURAL WONDER	Chesapeake Bay
TRAVEL TIP	Don't leave without trying Old Bay seasoning.

Aerial view of Calvert Cliffs at sunrise, MD

Cape Cod, MA

MASSACHUSETTS

BAY STATE

BEST TIME TO VISIT September–October

POPULAR ATTRACTIONS Boston · Cape Cod · Salem

HIDDEN GEMS Rockport · Martha's Vineyard · Nantucket

MUST EAT Clam Chowder

#1 FESTIVAL Head of the Charles Regatta

TOP NATURAL WONDER Cape Cod National Seashore

TRAVEL TIP Autumn is picture-perfect.

MICHIGAN

GREAT LAKES STATE

BEST TIME TO VISIT	June–September
POPULAR ATTRACTIONS	Detroit • Sleeping Bear Dunes • Mackinac Island
HIDDEN GEMS	Saugatuck • Pictured Rocks National Lakeshore • Holland
MUST EAT	Coney Dog
#1 FESTIVAL	Tulip Time Festival
TOP NATURAL WONDER	Pictured Rocks
TRAVEL TIP	Ferries = fun.

Pictured Rocks National Lakeshore, MI

Boundary Waters Canoe Area on John Lake, MN

MINNESOTA

NORTH STAR STATE

BEST TIME TO VISIT June–September

POPULAR ATTRACTIONS Minneapolis • Mall of America • Boundary Waters Canoe Area

HIDDEN GEMS Itasca State Park • Stillwater • Split Rock Lighthouse

MUST EAT Juicy Lucy Burger

#1 FESTIVAL Minnesota State Fair

TOP NATURAL WONDER Boundary Waters

TRAVEL TIP Bring bug spray.

MISSISSIPPI

MAGNOLIA STATE

BEST TIME TO VISIT	March–May
POPULAR ATTRACTIONS	Natchez · Jackson · Vicksburg National Military Park
HIDDEN GEMS	Ocean Springs · Tishomingo State Park · Oxford
MUST EAT	Catfish
#1 FESTIVAL	Mississippi Delta Blues Festival
TOP NATURAL WONDER	Natchez Trace Parkway
TRAVEL TIP	Southern charm everywhere.

Natchez Trace Parkway, MS

Overlooking Table Rock Lake, MO

MISSOURI

SHOW-ME STATE

BEST TIME TO VISIT May–September

POPULAR ATTRACTIONS St. Louis • Gateway Arch • Lake of the Ozarks

HIDDEN GEMS Hermann • Ste. Genevieve • Ha Ha Tonka State Park

MUST EAT Toasted Ravioli

#1 FESTIVAL St. Louis Mardi Gras

TOP NATURAL WONDER Ozark Mountains

TRAVEL TIP Gateway Arch = iconic photo.

MONTANA

TREASURE STATE

BEST TIME TO VISIT	June–September
POPULAR ATTRACTIONS	Glacier National Park • Yellowstone (Montana Side) • Missoula
HIDDEN GEMS	Bob Marshall Wilderness • Flathead Lake • Whitefish
MUST EAT	Bison Burger
#1 FESTIVAL	Big Sky Documentary Film Festival
TOP NATURAL WONDER	Glacier National Park
TRAVEL TIP	Big sky = big adventure.

Glacier National Park, MT

Chimney Rock, NE

NEBRASKA

CORNHUSKER STATE

BEST TIME TO VISIT May–September

POPULAR ATTRACTIONS Omaha · Lincoln · Henry Doorly Zoo

HIDDEN GEMS Sandhills · Chimney Rock · Valentine

MUST EAT Runza Sandwich

#1 FESTIVAL Nebraska State Fair

TOP NATURAL WONDER Chimney Rock

TRAVEL TIP Bring a hat—prairie sun waits for no one.

NEVADA

SILVER STATE

BEST TIME TO VISIT	March–May, September–November
POPULAR ATTRACTIONS	Las Vegas · Reno · Lake Tahoe
HIDDEN GEMS	Valley of Fire State Park · Great Basin National Park · Virginia City
MUST EAT	Shrimp Cocktail (Vegas classic)
#1 FESTIVAL	Burning Man
TOP NATURAL WONDER	Valley of Fire
TRAVEL TIP	Nights are neon, days are desert-hot.

Valley of Fire State Park, NV

Mount Washington, NH

NEW HAMPSHIRE

GRANITE STATE

BEST TIME TO VISIT September–October

POPULAR ATTRACTIONS Portsmouth • Mount Washington • Hanover

HIDDEN GEMS Franconia Notch State Park • North Conway • Lake Winnipesaukee

MUST EAT Apple Cider Donuts

#1 FESTIVAL Laconia Motorcycle Week

TOP NATURAL WONDER Mount Washington

TRAVEL TIP Fall foliage = mind-blowing.

NEW JERSEY

GARDEN STATE

BEST TIME TO VISIT May–September

POPULAR ATTRACTIONS Atlantic City · Princeton · Liberty State Park

HIDDEN GEMS Cape May · Delaware Water Gap · Red Bank

MUST EAT Pork Roll (Taylor Ham)

#1 FESTIVAL Atlantic City Airshow

TOP NATURAL WONDER Delaware Water Gap

TRAVEL TIP Salt air pairs well with boardwalk fries.

Delaware Water Gap viewed from Mount Tammany, NJ

Stairs extrance of Carlsbad Caverns, NM

NEW MEXICO

LAND OF ENCHANTMENT

BEST TIME TO VISIT March–May, September–October

POPULAR ATTRACTIONS Santa Fe • Albuquerque • Carlsbad Caverns

HIDDEN GEMS Taos Pueblo • Las Cruces • Bisti/De-Na-Zin Wilderness

MUST EAT Green Chile Stew

#1 FESTIVAL Albuquerque International Balloon Fiesta

TOP NATURAL WONDER Carlsbad Caverns

TRAVEL TIP High desert, high adventure.

NEW YORK

EMPIRE STATE

BEST TIME TO VISIT May–October

POPULAR ATTRACTIONS New York City · Niagara Falls · Buffalo

HIDDEN GEMS Hudson · Finger Lakes · Thousand Islands

MUST EAT Bagel & Lox

#1 FESTIVAL Film Festival

TOP NATURAL WONDER Niagara Falls

TRAVEL TIP The subway is your friend.

Central Park in New York City

Great Smoky Mountains National Park, NC

NORTH CAROLINA

TAR HEEL STATE

BEST TIME TO VISIT April–June, September–October

POPULAR ATTRACTIONS Asheville · Biltmore Estate · Outer Banks

HIDDEN GEMS Boone · Linville Gorge · New Bern

MUST EAT BBQ Pulled Pork

#1 FESTIVAL MerleFest

TOP NATURAL WONDER Great Smoky Mountains

TRAVEL TIP Mountains, beaches, repeat.

NORTH DAKOTA

PEACE GARDEN STATE

BEST TIME TO VISIT	June–September
POPULAR ATTRACTIONS	Fargo • Bismarck • Theodore Roosevelt National Park
HIDDEN GEMS	Medora • Enchanted Highway • Grand Forks
MUST EAT	Knoephla Soup
#1 FESTIVAL	Norsk Høstfest
TOP NATURAL WONDER	Badlands of Theodore Roosevelt NP
TRAVEL TIP	Embrace the wide-open skies.

Badlands of Theodore Roosevelt National Park, ND

Ash Cave in the Hocking Hills of Ohio

OHIO

BUCKEYE STATE

BEST TIME TO VISIT May–October

POPULAR ATTRACTIONS Cleveland · Columbus · Hocking Hills State Park

HIDDEN GEMS Yellow Springs · Sandusky · Cuyahoga Valley National Park

MUST EAT Pierogis

#1 FESTIVAL Ohio State Fair

TOP NATURAL WONDER Hocking Hills

TRAVEL TIP Don't underestimate small-town charm.

OKLAHOMA

SOONER STATE

BEST TIME TO VISIT	April–June, September–October
POPULAR ATTRACTIONS	Oklahoma City · Tulsa · Wichita Mountains Wildlife Refuge
HIDDEN GEMS	Guthrie · Beavers Bend State Park · Broken Bow
MUST EAT	Chicken-Fried Steak
#1 FESTIVAL	Oklahoma State Fair
TOP NATURAL WONDER	Wichita Mountains
TRAVEL TIP	Sunset skies = spectacular.

Wild Bison in Wichita Mountains Wildlife Refuge, OK

Crater Lake National Park, OR

OREGON

BEAVER STATE

BEST TIME TO VISIT June–September

POPULAR ATTRACTIONS Portland · Crater Lake National Park · Bend

HIDDEN GEMS Cannon Beach · Smith Rock State Park · Ashland

MUST EAT Marionberry Pie

#1 FESTIVAL Oregon Shakespeare Festival

TOP NATURAL WONDER Crater Lake

TRAVEL TIP Coffee first, cliffs second.

PENNSYLVANIA

KEYSTONE STATE

BEST TIME TO VISIT May–October

POPULAR ATTRACTIONS Philadelphia · Pittsburgh · Hersheypark

HIDDEN GEMS Jim Thorpe · Ricketts Glen State Park · Lancaster

MUST EAT Philly Cheesesteak

#1 FESTIVAL Kutztown Folk Festival

TOP NATURAL WONDER Ricketts Glen

TRAVEL TIP Chocolate lovers, rejoice.

Tuscarora Falls at Ricketts Glen State Park, PA

Block Island off Rhode Island's coast

RHODE ISLAND

OCEAN STATE

BEST TIME TO VISIT	May–September
POPULAR ATTRACTIONS	Newport · Providence · Block Island
HIDDEN GEMS	Bristol · Beavertail State Park · Watch Hill
MUST EAT	Clam Chowder
#1 FESTIVAL	Newport Jazz Festival
TOP NATURAL WONDER	Block Island
TRAVEL TIP	Smallest state, biggest charm.

SOUTH CAROLINA

PALMETTO STATE

BEST TIME TO VISIT	March–May, September–October
POPULAR ATTRACTIONS	Charleston • Myrtle Beach • Greenville
HIDDEN GEMS	Hunting Island State Park • Beaufort • Congaree National Park
MUST EAT	Shrimp and Grits
#1 FESTIVAL	Spoleto Festival USA
TOP NATURAL WONDER	Congaree Swamp
TRAVEL TIP	Don't skip the historic streets.

Congaree National Park, SC

Sunset at Badlands National Park, SD

SOUTH DAKOTA

MOUNT RUSHMORE STATE

BEST TIME TO VISIT May–September

POPULAR ATTRACTIONS Mount Rushmore • Badlands National Park • Sioux Falls

HIDDEN GEMS Deadwood • Custer State Park • Spearfish Canyon

MUST EAT Chislic

#1 FESTIVAL Sturgis Motorcycle Rally

TOP NATURAL WONDER Badlands

TRAVEL TIP Don't forget your camera.

TENNESSEE

VOLUNTEER STATE

BEST TIME TO VISIT March–May, September–October

POPULAR ATTRACTIONS Nashville · Memphis · Great Smoky Mountains

HIDDEN GEMS Gatlinburg · Pigeon Forge · Lookout Mountain

MUST EAT Barbecue Ribs

#1 FESTIVAL Bonnaroo

TOP NATURAL WONDER Great Smoky Mountains

TRAVEL TIP Music is in the air everywhere.

Great Smoky Mountains, TN

Big Bend National Park, TX

TEXAS

LONE STAR STATE

BEST TIME TO VISIT	March–May, September–November
POPULAR ATTRACTIONS	Austin · San Antonio · Big Bend National Park
HIDDEN GEMS	Fredericksburg · Marfa · Enchanted Rock
MUST EAT	Brisket
#1 FESTIVAL	South by Southwest (SXSW)
TOP NATURAL WONDER	Big Bend
TRAVEL TIP	BBQ and bluebonnets for days.

UTAH

BEEHIVE STATE

BEST TIME TO VISIT	April–May, September–October
POPULAR ATTRACTIONS	Arches National Park • Zion National Park • Salt Lake City
HIDDEN GEMS	Capitol Reef National Park • Bryce Canyon National Park • Moab
MUST EAT	Fry Sauce
#1 FESTIVAL	Sundance Film Festival
TOP NATURAL WONDER	Zion National Park
TRAVEL TIP	Red rocks, big thrills.

Slot Canyon in Zion National Park, UT

Gravel trail in Vermont's Green Mountains

VERMONT

GREEN MOUNTAIN STATE

BEST TIME TO VISIT September–October

POPULAR ATTRACTIONS Burlington · Montpelier · Stowe

HIDDEN GEMS Middlebury · Smugglers' Notch · Shelburne Farms

MUST EAT Maple Syrup

#1 FESTIVAL Vermont Maple Festival

TOP NATURAL WONDER Green Mountains

TRAVEL TIP Fall foliage perfection.

VIRGINIA

OLD DOMINION

BEST TIME TO VISIT April–June, September–October

POPULAR ATTRACTIONS Williamsburg • Richmond • Shenandoah National Park

HIDDEN GEMS Charlottesville • Luray Caverns • Abingdon

MUST EAT Ham Biscuits

#1 FESTIVAL Virginia Wine Festival

TOP NATURAL WONDER Shenandoah National Park

TRAVEL TIP Skyline Drive = scenic bliss.

Shenandoah National Park, VA

Mount Rainier over Puget Sound, WA

WASHINGTON

EVERGREEN STATE

BEST TIME TO VISIT June–September

POPULAR ATTRACTIONS Seattle · Mount Rainier National Park · Spokane

HIDDEN GEMS Leavenworth · San Juan Islands · Olympic National Park

MUST EAT Salmon

#1 FESTIVAL Seattle International Film Festival

TOP NATURAL WONDER Mount Rainier

TRAVEL TIP Coffee = mandatory.

WEST VIRGINIA

MOUNTAIN STATE

BEST TIME TO VISIT May–October

POPULAR ATTRACTIONS New River Gorge Bridge • Charleston • Seneca Rocks

HIDDEN GEMS Harpers Ferry • Dolly Sods Wilderness • Shepherdstown

MUST EAT Pepperoni Roll

#1 FESTIVAL Mountain State Forest Festival

TOP NATURAL WONDER New River Gorge

TRAVEL TIP Adventure awaits. Bring hiking boots.

New River Gorge and the New River, WV

Apostle Islands National Lakeshore, WI

WISCONSIN

BADGER STATE

BEST TIME TO VISIT June–September

POPULAR ATTRACTIONS Milwaukee · Madison · Door County

HIDDEN GEMS Bayfield · Apostle Islands · Kettle Moraine State Forest

MUST EAT Cheese Curds

#1 FESTIVAL Summerfest

TOP NATURAL WONDER Apostle Islands

TRAVEL TIP Dairy + lake = win-win.

WYOMING

EQUALITY STATE

BEST TIME TO VISIT June–September

POPULAR ATTRACTIONS Yellowstone National Park • Grand Teton National Park • Jackson

HIDDEN GEMS Bighorn Mountains • Fossil Butte National Monument • Sheridan

MUST EAT Bison Steak

#1 FESTIVAL Cheyenne Frontier Days

TOP NATURAL WONDER Yellowstone

TRAVEL TIP Big skies, bigger adventures.

Yellowstone National Park, WY

EXPLORE AMERICA'S NATIONAL PARKS

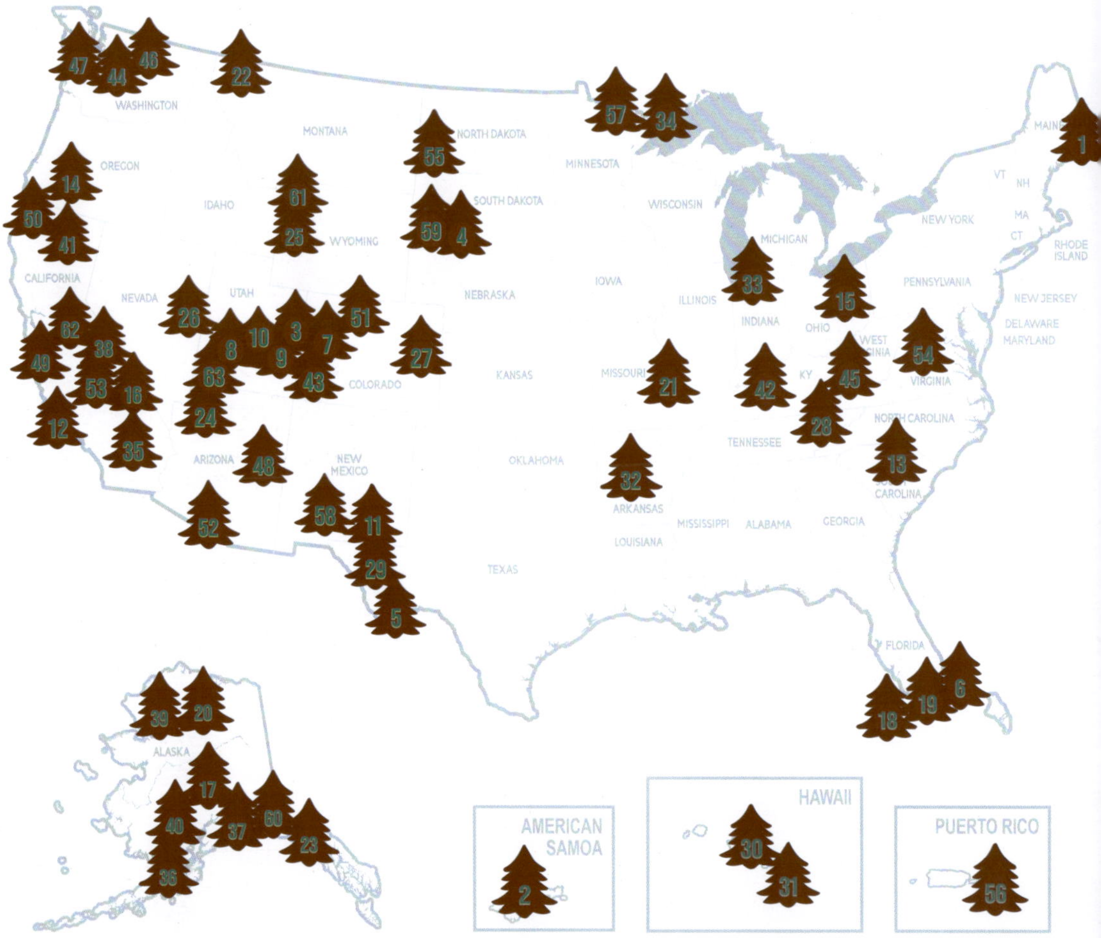

Scan the QR code for the latest U.S. National Park entry fees, updates, and details on annual and combo passes. If you plan to visit 3–4 major parks, the pass often pays for itself. Plus, nearly 20 parks offer free entry year-round (you'll find them in the link!).

ADVENTURE ARCHIVE

Scratch + check off the U.S. National Parks you've visited with a coin.

America's national parks protect the country's most remarkable natural treasures. **Use this map to find your next unforgettable destination.**

- ☐ 1. Acadia National Park (ME)
- ☐ 2. Arches National Park (UT)
- ☐ 3. Badlands National Park (SD)
- ☐ 4. Big Bend National Park (TX)
- ☐ 5. Biscayne National Park (FL)
- ☐ 6. Black Canyon of the Gunnison National Park (CO)
- ☐ 7. Bryce Canyon National Park (UT)
- ☐ 8. Canyonlands National Park (UT)
- ☐ 9. Capitol Reef National Park (UT)
- ☐ 10. Carlsbad Caverns National Park (NM)
- ☐ 11. Channel Islands National Park (CA)
- ☐ 12. Congaree National Park (SC)
- ☐ 13. Crater Lake National Park (OR)
- ☐ 14. Cuyahoga Valley National Park (OH)
- ☐ 15. Death Valley National Park (CA, NV)
- ☐ 16. Denali National Park (AK)
- ☐ 17. Dry Tortugas National Park (FL)
- ☐ 18. Everglades National Park (FL)
- ☐ 19. Gates of the Arctic National Park (AK)
- ☐ 20. Gateway Arch National Park (MO)
- ☐ 21. Glacier Bay National Park (AK)
- ☐ 22. Glacier National Park (MT)
- ☐ 23. Grand Canyon National Park (AZ)
- ☐ 24. Grand Teton National Park (WY)
- ☐ 25. Great Basin National Park (NV)
- ☐ 26. Great Sand Dunes National Park (CO)
- ☐ 27. Great Smoky Mountains National Park (NC, TN)
- ☐ 28. Guadalupe Mountains National Park (TX)
- ☐ 29. Haleakala National Park (HI)
- ☐ 30. Hawai'i Volcanoes National Park (HI)
- ☐ 31. Hot Springs National Park (AR)
- ☐ 32. Indiana Dunes National Park (IN)
- ☐ 33. Isle Royale National Park (MI)
- ☐ 34. Joshua Tree National Park (CA)
- ☐ 35. Katmai National Park (AK)
- ☐ 36. Kenai Fjords National Park (AK)
- ☐ 37. Kings Canyon National Park (CA)
- ☐ 38. Kobuk Valley National Park (AK)
- ☐ 39. Lake Clark National Park (AK)
- ☐ 40. Lassen Volcanic National Park (CA)
- ☐ 41. Mammoth Cave National Park (KY)
- ☐ 42. Mesa Verde National Park (CO)
- ☐ 43. Mount Rainier National Park (WA)
- ☐ 44. National Park of American Samoa (American Samoa)
- ☐ 45. New River Gorge National Park & Preserve (WV)
- ☐ 46. North Cascades National Park (WA)
- ☐ 47. Olympic National Park (WA)
- ☐ 48. Petrified Forest National Park (AZ)
- ☐ 49. Pinnacles National Park (CA)
- ☐ 50. Redwood National Park (CA)
- ☐ 51. Rocky Mountain National Park (CO)
- ☐ 52. Saguaro National Park (AZ)
- ☐ 53. Sequoia National Park (CA)
- ☐ 54. Shenandoah National Park (VA)
- ☐ 55. Theodore Roosevelt National Park (ND)
- ☐ 56. Virgin Islands National Park (U.S. Virgin Islands)
- ☐ 57. Voyageurs National Park (MN)
- ☐ 58. White Sands National Park (NM)
- ☐ 59. Wind Cave National Park (SD)
- ☐ 60. Wrangell–St. Elias National Park (AK)
- ☐ 61. Yellowstone National Park (WY, MT, ID)
- ☐ 62. Yosemite National Park (CA)
- ☐ 63. Zion National Park (UT)

CONTINENTS CONQUERED

Exploring every continent is a big goal — and for most people, it's pretty rare.

The average person has visited **about 2 continents** in their lifetime.

Only an estimated **5–10%** of people worldwide have visited 5 or more continents.

And it is estimated that **less than 1%** of the global population has been to all seven continents.

ADVENTURE ARCHIVE

Write down the year(s) you visited next to the continents.

How many continents have you visited?

Scratch off the continents you've visited.

WHEN TO SEE THE WORLD

SPRING
SUMMER
AUTUMN

NORTH AMERICA

Season: Fall
Best Month: October

Stunning foliage in many regions, comfortable temperatures, and a sweet spot between summer crowds and winter weather.

SOUTH AMERICA

Season: Spring
Best Month: October

Mild weather in the Andes, ideal conditions in Patagonia before peak season, and great timing for both rainforest and mountain exploration.

EUROPE

Season: Autumn
Month: September

Warm days, thinner crowds, harvest festivals, and beautiful countryside after the summer rush.

SEASONS AREN'T THE SAME EVERYWHERE

Seasons are opposite in each hemisphere because of the Earth's tilt. When it's summer in the north, it's winter in the south. So July means beaches in Europe and winter in Australia.

AFRICA

Season: Spring
Best Month: May

Dry conditions in many safari regions mean excellent wildlife viewing, comfortable temperatures, and fewer crowds before peak summer travel.

AUSTRALIA

Season: Autumn
Best Month: April

Mild weather, fewer tourists, and excellent conditions for exploring cities, coastlines, and the Outback without peak summer heat.

ASIA

Season: Spring
Best Month: April

Pleasant temperatures across much of the continent, cherry blossoms in East Asia, and ideal conditions before monsoon season begins in many regions.

ANTARCTICA

Season: Summer
Best Month: January

The warmest month of the year (still chilly!), with long daylight hours and prime penguin and whale activity.

ROAD TRIP INSPIRATION

THE ART OF THE OPEN ROAD

There's a moment on every road trip when something shifts. It might be when the city skyline disappears in your rearview mirror. Or when the radio station fades into static and the road stretches out in front of you like a blank page. That's when the trip really begins.

Road trips have a way of reminding us that travel doesn't always have to involve airports, boarding passes, or months of planning. Sometimes the best adventures start with nothing more than a full tank of gas and a loose idea of where you'd like to go.

If the idea of a road trip feels a little daunting, here's the good news: the best ones are rarely the most planned.

THE ONLY THINGS YOU REALLY NEED:

A DESTINATION
(OR AT LEAST A DIRECTION)

You don't need a perfect itinerary. Pick a place that excites you and let the journey fill in the rest.

A LOOSE ROUTE

Plot a few key stops, but leave room for detours. The roadside diner, scenic overlook, or odd little museum you didn't plan for will often become the highlight.

GREAT COMPANY
(OR GREAT SOLITUDE)

Road trips are about shared playlists, unexpected conversations, and long stretches of quiet thinking. All are equally valuable.

A SENSE OF CURIOSITY

Say yes to the strange roadside attraction. Pull over for the view. Take the extra 20-minute detour.

A FEW ROAD TRIP TRUTHS

- The best memories rarely happen on schedule.
- The most interesting towns are usually the ones you've never heard of.
- Scenic routes are almost always worth the extra time.
- Snacks improve everything.

A SIMPLE ROAD TRIP FORMULA

Not sure where to start? Try this...

RECOMMENDATION

3–4 hours of driving a day

1	+	1	=	1
memorable stop		local meal		perfect day on the road

Repeat for as many days as you like.

THE REAL MAGIC OF ROAD TRIPS

Road trips remind us that travel isn't just about the destination. It's about watching landscapes change mile by mile. It's about the music you'll forever associate with a certain stretch of highway. It's about discovering that the journey itself is the adventure.

So pick a direction.

Roll the windows down.

And see where the road takes you.

10 CLASSIC AMERICAN ROAD TRIPS

These are routes that have become legendary not just for the destinations they connect, but for the landscapes, towns, and unexpected stops along the way.

1. Pacific Coast Highway (California)

San Francisco → Big Sur → Santa Barbara → Los Angeles

Cliffs, ocean views, and some of the most dramatic coastal driving in the world.

2. Route 66

Chicago → Missouri → Oklahoma → Texas → New Mexico → Arizona → California

The original American road trip, filled with neon signs, diners, and roadside nostalgia.

3. Blue Ridge Parkway

Virginia → North Carolina

A slower, scenic drive through the Appalachian Mountains with endless overlooks.

4. Going-to-the-Sun Road

Glacier National Park, Montana

A breathtaking alpine drive through glaciers, mountain peaks, and wildlife habitat.

5. Utah's Mighty Five Loop

Zion → Bryce Canyon → Capitol Reef → Arches → Canyonlands

Red rock landscapes and some of the most surreal terrain in the United States.

ADVENTURE ARCHIVE

Check off the legendary routes you've taken or draw a star next to ones you want to.

6. Florida Keys Overseas Highway

Miami → Key West

A drive across turquoise water on bridges that stretch between tropical islands.

7. Great River Road

Minnesota → Louisiana

Follow the Mississippi River through historic river towns and changing landscapes.

8. Yellowstone & Grand Teton Loop

Wyoming / Montana / Idaho

Geysers, wildlife, and sweeping mountain scenery.

9. New England Fall Foliage Route

Vermont → New Hampshire → Maine

One of the most colorful drives in the country during autumn.

10. Alaska's Seward Highway

Anchorage → Seward

Glaciers, mountains, and wildlife around nearly every corner.

ROAD TRIP PACKING CHECKLIST

Road trips are easier when you pack for both **comfort and spontaneity.**

The goal isn't to pack everything. It's to pack enough so that when something interesting appears, you're ready to stop.

Check when packed!

ESSENTIALS

- ☐ Driver's license
- ☐ Car insurance / registration
- ☐ Phone charger
- ☐ Offline maps or downloaded GPS
- ☐ Sunglasses

COMFORT

- ☐ Refillable water bottle
- ☐ Snacks
- ☐ Travel blanket
- ☐ Neck pillow
- ☐ Comfortable walking shoes

ROAD TRIP READY

- ☐ Cooler or insulated bag
- ☐ Reusable shopping bags
- ☐ Hand wipes / sanitizer
- ☐ Small first-aid kit
- ☐ Flashlight

ADVENTURE EXTRAS

- ☐ Camera
- ☐ Journal or travel notebook (this book)
- ☐ Deck of cards
- ☐ National park pass
- ☐ Picnic blanket

ROAD TRIP PLAYLIST CONCEPT

ADVENTURE ARCHIVE
Write in your own evolving roadtrip songs and make them your tradition.

Every great road trip deserves the perfect soundtrack. Set the tone with a playlist that fits your vibe—by decade, genre, or mood. Dive into a favorite artist's discography, queue up a podcast, or take turns sharing songs with your travel companions.

For an even richer experience, let your music evolve with the journey, matching the changing landscapes, energy, and moments along the way.

DEPARTURE SONGS *For the moment the trip begins.*

- "Here Comes the Sun" – The Beatles
- "Send Me On My Way" – Rusted Root

♪ ______________________

♪ ______________________

HIGHWAY SONGS *For long stretches of open road.*

- "Life Is a Highway" – Tom Cochrane
- "Take It Easy" – Eagles

♪ ______________________

♪ ______________________

SUNSET DRIVING SONGS *When the light gets golden and the miles slow down.*

- "Dreams" – Fleetwood Mac
- "Fast Car" – Tracy Chapman

♪ ______________________

♪ ______________________

ARRIVAL SONGS *For when you finally reach your destination.*

- "Home" – Edward Sharpe & The Magnetic Zeros
- "On Top of the World" – Imagine Dragons

♪ ______________________

♪ ______________________

ROAD TRIP GAMES & PROMPTS

Road trips have a way of turning small moments into big memories. These simple games keep the journey entertaining.

LICENSE PLATE HUNT

See how many different states you can spot along the way.

ROAD TRIP QUESTIONS

Ask one question every hour:

- **What place in the world do you want to visit most?**
- **What would your dream road trip look like?**
- **If you could live in any town we pass, where would it be?**

THE ALPHABET GAME

Find every letter of the alphabet in order using road signs and billboards.

STORY BUILDER

One person starts a story with one sentence. Each passenger adds another sentence as the miles go by.

LOCAL FOOD CHALLENGE

At every stop, try something the region is known for.

FUN IDEA: Pack a small toy or pick up one on your journey. Take silly photos of it in every place you stop.

ROAD TRIP BINGO

Road trips are full of small surprises. This bingo card turns the journey into a game. Mark a square whenever you see one of these along the road. Try to get **five in a row**, or challenge yourself to complete the entire board.

ADVENTURE ARCHIVE

Use markings or small stickers so you can restart fresh every trip.

Welcome to a new state sign	Roadside fruit stand	Historic town square	Scenic overlook	Wind farm
Vintage motel sign	Giant roadside statue	Covered bridge	Local diner	Classic pickup truck
National park entrance sign	Small town parade	**FREE SPACE** Windows down moment	Old railroad crossing	Local craft shop
Lighthouse	Farmers market	Hot air balloon	Scenic mountain pass	Street mural
Wild animals crossing sign	Old gas station	Sunset over the highway	Vintage neon sign	Waterfall

BEST ROAD TRIP SNACKS BY REGION

EVERY REGION OF THE COUNTRY HAS SOMETHING DELICIOUS WORTH PULLING OVER FOR

WEST COAST

- Fish tacos
- Avocados or guacamole
- Fresh berries
- Sourdough bread

SOUTHWEST

- Green chile burritos
- Street tacos
- Tamales
- Churros

MIDWEST

- Cheese curds
- Butter burgers
- Cherry pie
- Sweet corn

SOUTH

- Fried chicken
- Pecan pie
- Boiled peanuts
- Barbecue sandwiches

NORTHEAST

- Lobster rolls
- Maple donuts
- Apple cider
- Soft pretzels

"It doesn't matter how old you are, buying snacks for a road trip should always look like an unsupervised 9-year-old was given $100."

THE UNIVERSAL ROAD TRIP SNACK KIT

Every car should have:

- **Jerky**
- **Chocolate**
- **Chips**
- **Fresh fruit**
- **Sparkling water**
- **Something sweet for the late-night drive**

TRAVEL TIP: Regional snacks make great souvenirs to bring back to family and friends. Nothing says "thank you for watching my dog" like a box of assorted fudge.

50 UNEXPECTED ROADSIDE ATTRACTIONS WORTH STOPPING FOR

ARIZONA

- ☐ The Center of the World - Felicity, AZ
- ☐ The Wigwam Motel - Holbrook, AZ

CALIFORNIA

- ☐ Salvation Mountain - Niland, CA
- ☐ Mystery Spot - Santa Cruz, CA
- ☐ The Cabazon Dinosaurs - Cabazon, CA
- ☐ The Bottle Tree Ranch - Oro Grande, CA
- ☐ The International Banana Museum - Mecca, CA

COLORADO

- ☐ The UFO Watchtower - Hooper, CO

FLORIDA

- ☐ The World's Largest Rubber Band Ball – Ripley's Believe It or Not! - Orlando, FL

GEORGIA

- ☐ The World's Largest Peanut - Ashburn, GA
- ☐ The Big Chicken - Marietta, GA

ILLINOIS

- ☐ The World's Largest Ketchup Bottle - Collinsville, IL
- ☐ The Pink Elephant Antique Mall - Livingston, IL
- ☐ The World's Largest Wind Chime - Casey, IL

KANSAS

- ☐ The World's Largest Ball of Twine - Cawker City, KS

MAINE

- ☐ The Giant Lobster (Big Lobster) - Rockland, ME
- ☐ The Desert of Maine - Freeport, ME

MASSACHUSETTS

- ☐ The Paper House - Rockport, MA

MINNESOTA

- ☐ The Jolly Green Giant Statue - Blue Earth, MN
- ☐ The Spam Museum - Austin, MN
- ☐ The Giant Paul Bunyan Statue - Bemidji, MN

MISSOURI

- ☐ The World's Largest Rocking Chair - Cuba, MO
- ☐ The World's Largest Fork - Springfield, MO

MONTANA

- ☐ The Garden of One Thousand Buddhas - Arlee, MT

NEBRASKA

- ☐ Carhenge - Alliance, NE

ADVENTURE ARCHIVE

Check off the roadside attractions you've visited. Write in others you've discovered.

Some of the best stops aren't famous. They're the weird museum, the hand-painted sign, or the giant statue someone built just because they could.

The rule of road trips is simple:
If it makes you laugh or wonder what it is — pull over.

NEVADA

- ☐ The Shoe Tree - near Middlegate, NV
- ☐ The Goldwell Open Air Museum - near Beatty, NV
- ☐ The Ghost Town of Rhyolite - Rhyolite, NV

NEW JERSEY

- ☐ Lucy the Elephant - Margate City, NJ

NEW MEXICO

- ☐ The International UFO Museum - Roswell, NM
- ☐ The World's Largest Pistachio - Alamogordo, NM

NORTH CAROLINA

- ☐ The World's Largest Chest of Drawers - High Point, NC

NORTH DAKOTA

- ☐ The Enchanted Highway Sculptures - Regent, ND

OKLAHOMA

- ☐ The Blue Whale of Catoosa - Catoosa, OK

OREGON

- ☐ The Oregon Vortex - Gold Hill, OR

PENNSYLVANIA

- ☐ Roadside America Miniature Village - Shartlesville, PA
- ☐ The Giant Coffee Pot - Bedford, PA
- ☐ The Shoe House - York, PA

SOUTH DAKOTA

- ☐ The Corn Palace - Mitchell, SD
- ☐ Wall Drug - Wall, SD
- ☐ The Dinosaur Park - Rapid City, SD
- ☐ The Giant Prairie Dog Statue - near Badlands National Park, SD

TEXAS

- ☐ Cadillac Ranch - Amarillo, TX
- ☐ The World's Largest Cowboy Boots - San Antonio, TX
- ☐ The Big Texan Steak Ranch - Amarillo, TX

VIRGINIA

- ☐ Foamhenge - Natural Bridge, VA

WASHINGTON

- ☐ The Fremont Troll - Seattle, WA
- ☐ The Fremont Rocket - Seattle, WA

WEST VIRGINIA

- ☐ The Mystery Hole - Ansted, WV

WISCONSIN

- ☐ The House on the Rock -Spring Green, WI

UNFORGETTABLE ROAD TRIPS

Road Trip: ______________________________

Date: ______________________________

Memories to Keep: ______________________________

Road Trip: ______________________________

Date: ______________________________

Memories to Keep: ______________________________

Road Trip: ______________________________

Date: ______________________________

Memories to Keep: ______________________________

Road Trip: ______________________________

Date: ______________________________

Memories to Keep: ______________________________

ADVENTURE ARCHIVE

Don't forget to write about colorful characters you met along the way.

Road Trip: ______

Date: ______

Memories to Keep: ______

______

______

Road Trip: ______

Date: ______

Memories to Keep: ______

______

______

Road Trip: ______

Date: ______

Memories to Keep: ______

______

______

Road Trip: ______

Date: ______

Memories to Keep: ______

______

______

FESTIVALS IN THE U.S. THAT YOU CAN'T MISS

Every corner of the U.S. has traditions worth celebrating. From food festivals and cultural heritage celebrations to music gatherings and seasonal traditions, festivals offer one of the most memorable ways to experience a place. Planning a trip around a festival adds energy to travel: The streets feel alive, the food is unforgettable, and the local culture shines as it invites you in.

Here are some of the most unique and beloved festivals across the country.

WHERE TRADITION MEETS FUN

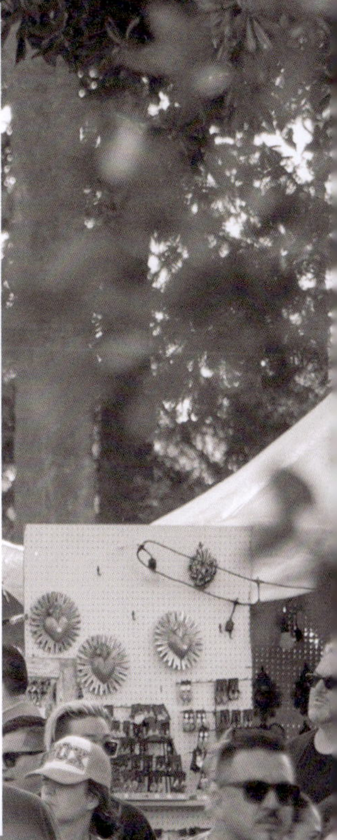

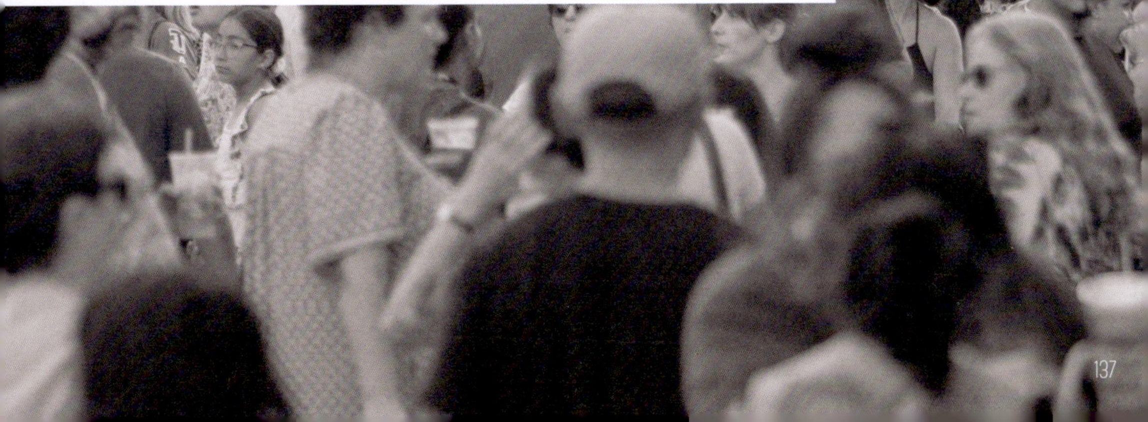

U.S. FESTIVALS WORTH EXPERIENCING (FOR ADULTS)

1. Sundance Film Festival — Park City, Utah
When: Late January (typically the last 10 days)
A leading film festival where indie films premiere amid Park City's snowy mountains.

2. Mardi Gras New Orleans — New Orleans, LA
When: February–March (peaks on Fat Tuesday, ~47 days before Easter)
Parades, jazz, and elaborate floats make Mardi Gras one of America's most iconic celebrations.

3. St. Patrick's Day Chicago — Chicago, IL
When: March 17 (parade usually the Saturday before)
The Chicago River famously turns bright green as the city celebrates Irish heritage.

4. South by Southwest — Austin, TX
When: Mid-March (about 9–10 days)
A massive celebration of music, technology, film, and creative culture.

5. National Cherry Blossom Festival — Washington, D.C.
When: Late March–Early April (aligned with peak bloom)
Spring arrives in spectacular fashion when thousands of cherry blossoms bloom around the Tidal Basin.

FESTIVAL TRAVEL TIP: The best way to experience a festival is to **stay an extra day or two**. Explore the surrounding town, try the local food, and wander away from the main event. Soak it in.

Check when completed!

6. Kentucky Derby Festival — Louisville, KY
When: Mid-April–Early May (ends first Saturday in May)
Two weeks of celebrations leading up to the most famous horse race in the world.

7. New Orleans Jazz & Heritage Festival — New Orleans, LA
When: Last weekend of April + first weekend of May
A legendary music festival celebrating jazz, blues, and the rich culture of New Orleans.

8. Burning Man — Black Rock Desert, NV
When: Last Sunday in August through Labor Day
A temporary city rises in the desert for a week of art, creativity, music, and radical self-expression.

9. Aloha Festivals — Across Hawaii
When: Throughout September (major events mid-month)
Traditional Hawaiian music, dance, and cultural celebrations honoring the spirit of aloha.

10. Albuquerque International Balloon Fiesta — Albuquerque, NM
When: First full week of October
Hundreds of colorful hot-air balloons fill the sunrise sky in a breathtaking spectacle.

TOP 20 KID-FRIENDLY FESTIVALS IN THE UNITED STATES

Festivals can be magical for children — giant balloons in the sky, colorful parades, music in the streets, and food you can eat with your hands. These festivals combine **big visual moments, outdoor fun, and family-friendly activities**, making them perfect for travelers with kids.

☐ **1. Mardi Gras Family Parades — New Orleans, LA**
When: (Spring) February–Early March
Many daytime parades are family-friendly with colorful floats, costumes, and music.

☐ **2. St. Patrick's Day Parade — Chicago, IL**
When: (Spring) Mid-March
The Chicago River turns bright green while the city celebrates with one of the most festive parades in the country.

☐ **3. Frozen Dead Guy Days — Estes Park, CO**
When: (Spring) March
Embrace the quirky side of winter with offbeat fun, from coffin races to icy plunges, all set against a snowy mountain backdrop.

☐ **4. National Cherry Blossom Festival — Washington, D.C.**
When: (Spring) Late March–Early April
Springtime celebrations include parades, cultural performances, and the popular Blossom Kite Festival.

Check when completed!

5. Skagit Valley Tulip Festival — Skagit Valley, WA
When: (Spring) April
Miles of bright tulip fields create one of the most colorful spring experiences in the country.

6. Tulip Time Festival — Holland, MI
When: (Spring) Early May
Dutch traditions, colorful parades, and millions of tulips blooming throughout the town.

7. California State Fair — Sacramento, CA
When: (Summer) Mid–Late July
A classic American fair with rides, animals, live entertainment, and plenty of treats.

8. National Balloon Classic — Indianola, IA
When: (Summer) Late July–Early August
Hot-air balloons drift across the Midwestern sky with family activities and evening balloon glows.

9. Washington State International Kite Festival — Long Beach, WA
When: (Summer) August
Massive colorful kites soar over the coast while kids fly their own creations.

10. Gilroy Garlic Festival — Gilroy, CA
When: (Summer) Late July
Food demonstrations, cooking competitions, and family entertainment celebrate the famous garlic harvest.

KID-FRIENDLY U.S. FESTIVALS CONTINUED...

11. Aloha Festivals — Across Hawaii
When: (Fall) September

Traditional Hawaiian music, dance, parades, and cultural demonstrations celebrate island heritage.

12. Colorado Springs Labor Day Lift Off — Colorado Springs, CO
When: (Fall) Labor Day Weekend (early September)

A beautiful sunrise event where balloons rise over the Rocky Mountains.

13. National Folk Festival — Rotating U.S. cities
When: (Fall) September

A celebration of music, crafts, storytelling, and cultural traditions from across the country.

14. Albuquerque International Balloon Fiesta — Albuquerque, NM
When: (Fall) Early October

Hundreds of hot-air balloons fill the sky at sunrise, including whimsical animals and cartoon characters.

15. National Apple Harvest Festival — Arendtsville, PA
When: (Fall) Early October

Classic fall fun with hayrides, apple picking, handmade crafts, and warm apple cider.

FESTIVAL TIP FOR FAMILIES: Choose festivals with daytime activites. Arrive early, pack snacks, scout kid-friendly areas, and remember: **sometimes the best moments happen between the main events.**

Check when completed!

16. Keene Pumpkin Festival — Keene, NH
When: (Fall) October
Thousands of glowing jack-o'-lanterns create a spectacular fall display.

17. Texas Renaissance Festival — Todd Mission, TX
When: (Fall) October–November
A medieval village comes alive with jousting, costumes, crafts, and theatrical performances.

18. Pasadena Tournament of Roses Parade — Pasadena, CA
When: (Winter) January 1
Giant flower-covered floats roll through Pasadena on New Year's Day. One of America's most famous parades.

19. Epcot International Festival of the Arts — Orlando, FL
When: (Winter) January–February
Interactive art, music, and food experiences that are perfect for curious young travelers.

20. National Cowboy Poetry Gathering — Elko, Nevada
When: (Winter) Late January
Storytelling, music, and cowboy culture offer a unique glimpse into the American West.

CULTURE IN MOTION: FESTIVALS ACROSS THE GLOBE

Some of the most unforgettable travel experiences don't happen at landmarks. They happen in the middle of a celebration.

A street filled with music.
Lanterns glowing in the night sky.
The smell of food drifting through a crowded market.

Festivals are where culture comes alive. They offer a glimpse into traditions, stories, and communities that have often been celebrated for generations.

If you want to understand a place, visit when the locals are celebrating something meaningful.

Here are some of the world's most vibrant cultural festivals worth planning a trip around.

Check when completed!

1. Chinese New Year

Where: China and worldwide
When: Late January–February (varies with lunar calendar)

Celebrate the lunar new year with parades, lanterns, dragon dances, and dazzling fireworks. A vibrant mix of tradition and festivity.

2. Carnival

Where: Rio de Janeiro, Brazil
When: February–March (dates vary with Easter)

Rio erupts in music, dance, and dazzling costumes as samba schools compete in all-night parades, making this one of the world's most spectacular celebrations.

3. HOLI

Where: India
When: March

Known as the Festival of Colors, Holi welcomes spring with joyful chaos, vibrant powders, music, and playful celebration of friendship and renewal.

4. SONGKRAN

Where: Thailand
When: April

Thailand's New Year comes alive with massive water fights, symbolizing cleansing and starting fresh. Fun for locals and visitors alike.

5. EDINBURGH FESTIVAL FRINGE

Where: Edinburgh, Scotland
When: August

The world's largest arts festival, with thousands of performers taking over the city for comedy, theater, music, and more. Endless creativity and excitement.

6. LA TOMATINA

Where: Buñol, Spain
When: Last Wednesday in August

Join thousands in the world's biggest tomato fight, a messy, joyful, and unforgettable celebration of fun.

7. Oktoberfest

Where: Munich, Germany
When: Late September–First Weekend in October

Germany's iconic festival of beer, traditional music, and hearty food brings locals and travelers together in a lively Bavarian celebration.

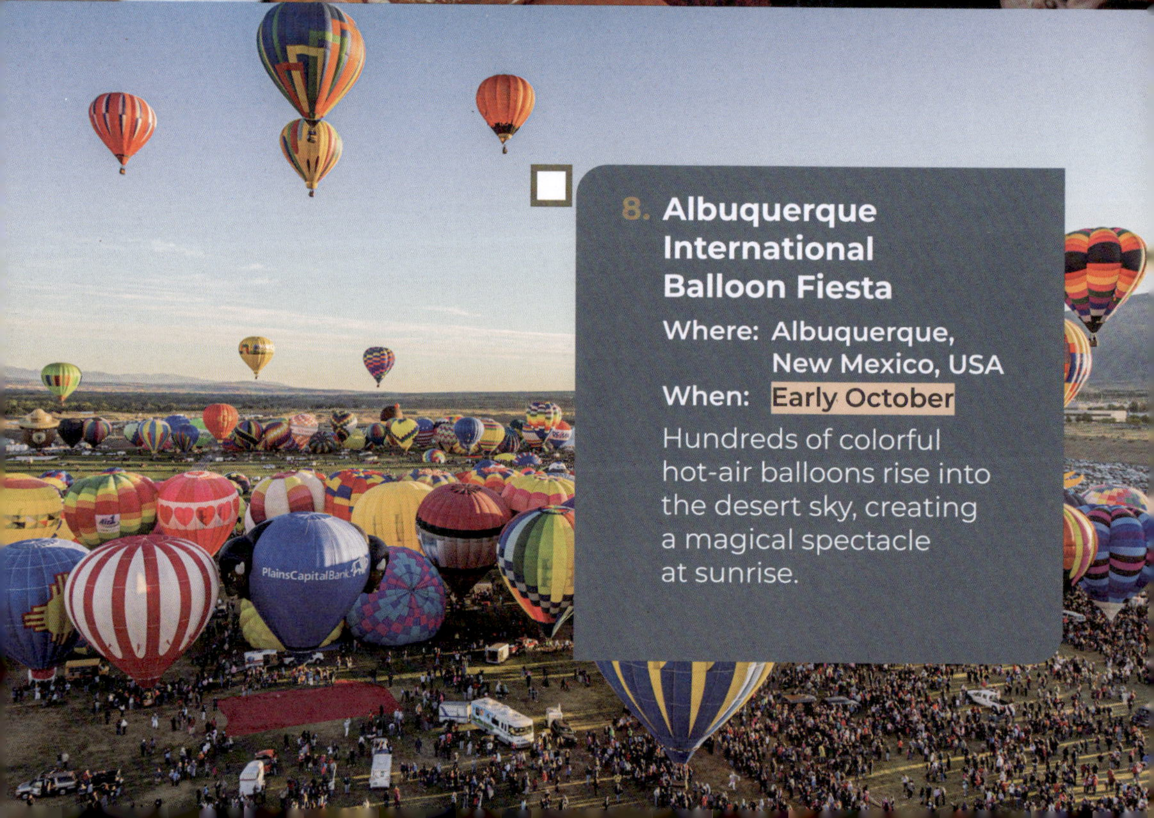

8. Albuquerque International Balloon Fiesta

Where: Albuquerque, New Mexico, USA
When: Early October

Hundreds of colorful hot-air balloons rise into the desert sky, creating a magical spectacle at sunrise.

9. Diwali

Where: India
When: October–November (dates vary with lunar calendar)

Cities and villages glow with candles, lanterns, and fireworks as families celebrate light, joy, and togetherness.

10. Day of the Dead

Where: Mexico
When: November 1–2

Families honor loved ones with colorful altars, marigolds, music, and lively celebrations blending remembrance with festive joy.

TIPS & TRICKS FOR THE PERFECT FESTIVAL TRIP

Festivals are some of the most joyful travel experiences you can have. They can also be long days filled with crowds, weather surprises, and lots of walking. A little preparation makes it easier to relax and fully enjoy the celebration.

Think of your festival plan in three simple layers: what to bring with you, what to keep nearby, and what to leave waiting for you when the day ends.

WHAT TO PACK IN YOUR DAY BAG

Check when packed!

- ☐ **Small crossbody or backpack**
  Hands-free is best when moving through crowds.
- ☐ **Portable phone charger**
  Photos, maps, and messaging can drain your battery faster than you expect.
- ☐ **Refillable water bottle**
  Many festivals have refill stations, and staying hydrated makes the whole day better.
- ☐ **Sunscreen**
  Even cloudy days can turn into long hours in the sun.
- ☐ **Cash and a credit card**
  Some vendors are cash-only, especially at smaller festivals.
- ☐ **Hand wipes or sanitizer**
  Street food is part of the fun, but clean hands make it better.
- ☐ **Light layer or scarf**
  Temperatures can drop quickly once the sun goes down.

WHAT TO KEEP IN THE CAR (OR NEARBY)

- ☐ **Comfortable backup shoes**
  If you've been standing all day, switching shoes can feel like a luxury.
- ☐ **Extra water and snacks**
  Great for the drive back or when food lines are long.
- ☐ **Portable cooler**
  Perfect for drinks or fresh fruit.
- ☐ **Blanket or foldable chairs**
  Ideal for outdoor concerts or grassy festival grounds.
- ☐ **Umbrella or poncho**
  Weather changes quickly, and festivals rarely pause for rain.

WHAT TO LEAVE AT THE HOTEL

- ☐ **Comfortable clothes**
  Changing into something soft and relaxed makes the evening feel complete.
- ☐ **Pain reliever and blister bandages**
  Your feet may thank you later.
- ☐ **Reusable tote bag**
  Useful for carrying souvenirs, local crafts, or festival merchandise.
- ☐ **A small laundry bag**
  Helpful if you've been dancing, walking, or celebrating all day.

FESTIVAL SURVIVAL GUIDE

ARRIVE EARLY
You'll avoid the biggest crowds and see more of the festival.

EAT WHEN LINES ARE SHORT
Food lines grow quickly once performances or events begin.

SET A MEETING POINT
If you're with friends, pick a landmark in case phones lose service.

EXPECT CROWDS
Arrive early for events and leave extra time for travel.

WANDER AWAY FROM THE MAIN STAGE
Some of the most memorable discoveries happen in smaller corners of the festival.

DON'T TRY TO SEE EVERYTHING
Festivals are meant to be experienced slowly: tasting food, listening to music drifting down the street, and stumbling upon moments you never planned. Leave space for the unexpected.

FESTIVALS ATTENDED

Festival: ______________________________

Date: ______________________________

Memories to Keep: ______________________________

____

____

Festival: ______________________________

Date: ______________________________

Memories to Keep: ______________________________

____

____

Festival: ______________________________

Date: ______________________________

Memories to Keep: ______________________________

____

____

Festival: ______________________________

Date: ______________________________

Memories to Keep: ______________________________

____

____

ADVENTURE ARCHIVE

What one thing do you wish you could have brought back home with you?

Festival: ______________________

Date: ______________________

Memories to Keep: ______________________

____

____

Festival: ______________________

Date: ______________________

Memories to Keep: ______________________

____

____

Festival: ______________________

Date: ______________________

Memories to Keep: ______________________

____

____

Festival: ______________________

Date: ______________________

Memories to Keep: ______________________

____

____

FOLLOW THE GAMES

TRAVEL THE WORLD THROUGH THE OLYMPICS

The Olympic Games are more than just a global sporting event. They're an incredible way to explore the world. Every four years, the Games move to a new host city, giving travelers the chance to experience different cultures, landmarks, and traditions while celebrating the spirit of international competition.

Planning trips around the Olympics can turn travel into a global adventure. From historic cities to modern capitals, each host destination offers its own flavor of food, festivals, and local pride. You might wander the ancient streets of Athens, explore the vibrant neighborhoods of Rio de Janeiro, or experience the electric energy of Tokyo during the Games.

Even if you don't attend events, visiting past or future Olympic host cities is a fun way to theme your travels. Many stadiums, Olympic parks, and athlete villages remain open to the public and become iconic landmarks long after the closing ceremony.

GO FOR GOLD: OLYMPIC TRAVEL TIPS

Important Tip: Olympic tickets go first to lottery winners, then general sales, and finally through official resellers. **Always buy from authorized sources to avoid scams.**

Plan Early
Book flights and hotels months ahead to lock in the best spots.

Smart Lodging
Staying a short walk or transit ride from venues can save time and money.

Use Public Transit
Metro, trains, and buses are faster than driving during the Games.

Expect Crowds
Arrive early for events and leave extra time for travel.

Pack Light & Smart
Comfortable shoes, weather gear, sunscreen, and water are essentials.

Stay Hydrated
Especially in summer, rest, drink often, and consider travel insurance.

Bring Your Spirit
Small items from home make great icebreakers with fellow fans.

Explore the City
Museums, parks, and local culture make the trip unforgettable.

☀ Summer Games / ❄ Winter Games

PAST OLYMPIC HOST CITIES

- 1896 – Athens ☀
- 1900 – Paris ☀
- 1904 – St. Louis ☀
- 1908 – London ☀
- 1912 – Stockholm ☀
- 1920 – Antwerp ☀
- 1924 – Paris ☀ / Chamonix ❄
- 1928 – Amsterdam ☀ / St. Moritz ❄
- 1932 – Los Angeles ☀ / Lake Placid ❄
- 1936 – Berlin ☀ / Garmisch-Partenkirchen ❄
- 1948 – London ☀ / St. Moritz ❄
- 1952 – Helsinki ☀ / Oslo ❄
- 1956 – Melbourne ☀ / Cortina d'Ampezzo ❄
- 1960 – Rome ☀ / Squaw Valley ❄
- 1964 – Tokyo ☀ / Innsbruck ❄
- 1968 – Mexico City ☀ / Grenoble ❄
- 1972 – Munich ☀ / Sapporo ❄
- 1976 – Montreal ☀ / Innsbruck ❄
- 1980 – Moscow ☀ / Lake Placid ❄
- 1984 – Los Angeles ☀ / Sarajevo ❄
- 1988 – Seoul ☀ / Calgary ❄
- 1992 – Barcelona ☀ / Albertville ❄
- 1994 – Lillehammer ❄
- 1996 – Atlanta ☀
- 1998 – Nagano ❄
- 2000 – Sydney ☀
- 2002 – Salt Lake City ❄
- 2004 – Athens ☀
- 2006 – Turin ❄
- 2008 – Beijing ☀
- 2010 – Vancouver ❄
- 2012 – London ☀
- 2014 – Sochi ❄
- 2016 – Rio de Janeiro ☀
- 2018 – Pyeongchang ❄
- 2020 – Tokyo ☀ (held 2021)
- 2022 – Beijing ❄
- 2024 – Paris ☀

Fun Tip: Bring extra pins and trade early. It's one of the most fun ways to meet fellow fans and make lasting Olympic memories!

2026 – Milano-Cortina, Italy ❄

2028 – Los Angeles, USA ☀

2030 – French Alps, France ❄

2032 – Brisbane, Australia ☀

2034 – Salt Lake City, USA ❄

Fun Fact: The 2028 Los Angeles Games (LA28) are notable for being the first in 80 years to use only existing venues, including SoFi Stadium for the opening ceremony and swimming. Scan the QR code to learn more about the LA28 Games.

SAVE SMARTER, TRAVEL FURTHER

STRETCH YOUR DOLLAR AROUND THE WORLD

1. SET A TRAVEL GOAL

Decide where you want to go and how much you'll need. Having a clear target makes saving tangible.

2. MAKE A TRAVEL BUDGET

Track your expenses, cut unnecessary spending, and figure out how much you can put aside each month. Even small amounts add up.

3. OPEN A TRAVEL FUND

Keep your travel money separate—like a dedicated savings account or jar. Watching it grow is motivating.

4. AUTOMATE SAVINGS

Set up automatic transfers each paycheck so saving happens without thinking about it.

5. HUNT FOR DEALS

Use fare alerts, off-season travel, and loyalty programs to stretch your money further.

6. EARN EXTRA TRAVEL CASH

Side gigs, freelancing, or selling unused items can give your travel fund a boost.

7. KEEP YOUR EYE ON THE PRIZE

Visualize your trip. Pin maps, save photos, or create a travel countdown. Motivation makes saving fun.

TRAVEL MONEY TIP: Skip airport exchange counters. Use a local ATM or bank for better rates and lower fees.

TRAVEL PLANNING
WHERE TO START

THE ART OF GOING SOMEWHERE NEW

Not all trips begin with a destination.
Some begin with a feeling.

Copy these questions into a notebook or type them into a blank document and answer them. Writing down the answers will help shape what this journey means to you and, before you know it, your itinerary will begin to take form.

1. DESTINATION

Where are you going, and what drew you there? Social media is a great place to discover travel inspiration. Search a destination and let the algorithm take it from there.

2. DATES

When does this chapter begin and end? (Best season to travel there, events that might play a role in the decision. Use this book!)

3. INTENTION FOR THIS TRIP

What do you want more of? (Rest, adventure, connection, discovery, stillness, summer memories, escape)

4. MUST-EXPERIENCE MOMENTS

A few things you don't want to miss. (Events, great landmarks, movie moments, and anything that inspired you to visit this destination)

PREFER LESS PLANNING?

Group tours handle the details so you can simply enjoy the journey.

5. WHERE YOU'LL STAY

A place to land, recharge, and dream. Defining your desires first can help in the final selection of hotels, rentals, or staying with family. (Be mindful of amenities you might require like cooking to eat for dietary restrictions, laundry, proximity to public transit)

6. WHAT YOU'LL BRING

Not just what you pack, but also what to carry with you.

- Essentials:
- Something meaningful:
- Something just for joy:

INTERNATIONAL TRAVEL RULE:

Make sure your passport expiration date is at least six months beyond your planned return date.

7. IF PLANS CHANGE (YOUR EXIT STRATEGY)

Sometimes the unexpected calls you home, or somewhere else entirely. And sometimes, a place simply isn't what you hoped it would be, and you need out. Give yourself permission to pivot.

- Who would you contact if you needed to return early?
- What are your quickest routes home?
- Do you have flexible bookings or backup options?

A gentle reminder: You are never stuck. You can always choose differently.

8. A THOUGHT BEFORE YOU GO

What are you hoping to find… or leave behind?

SPEAK A LITTLE, CONNECT A LOT

Travel is more than the sights—it's the people. Learning key words like Hello, Goodbye, Please, Thank You, Cheers, and Bathroom in the world's most-learned languages makes every interaction smoother, shows respect, and turns strangers into friends. These six words are your passport to connection.

HERE ARE 6 USEFUL PHRASES IN THE TOP 13 LEARNED LANGUAGES

HELLO!

LANGUAGE	PRONUNCIATION (ENGLISH)
English	**HEL-loh**
Spanish	**OH-lah**
French	**bon-ZHOOR**
German	**HAH-loh**
Japanese	**kon-NEE-chee-wah**
Mandarin Chinese	**NEE how**
Italian	**chow**
Portuguese	**oh-LAH**
Korean	**AHN-nyung-ha-seh-yo**
Russian	**pree-VYET**
Arabic	**MAR-ha-bah**
Hindi	**nuh-MUS-tey**
Dutch	**HAH-loh**

TRAVEL TIP: Smile, say hello, and show respect. That goes farther than perfect pronunciation!

GOODBYE!

LANGUAGE	PRONUNCIATION (ENGLISH)
English	good-BYE
Spanish	ah-dee-OHS
French	oh ruh-VWAHR
German	owf VEE-der-zay-en
Japanese	sah-yo-NAH-rah
Mandarin Chinese	ZAI jyen
Italian	ah-ree-veh-DER-chee
Portuguese	ah-DEH-oos
Korean	ahn-nyung-hee gah-seh-yo
Russian	doh svee-DAH-nee-yuh
Arabic	mah-ah sah-LAH-mah
Hindi	al-vi-DAH
Dutch	tot ZEENS

TRAVEL TIP: A friendly smile and a polite goodbye leave a lasting impression anywhere in the world.

PLEASE.

LANGUAGE	PRONUNCIATION (ENGLISH)
English	pleez
Spanish	por fah-VOR
French	seel voo PLEH
German	BIT-uh
Japanese	oh-neh-guy shee-mas
Mandarin Chinese	ching
Italian	per fah-VOH-reh
Portuguese	por fah-VOR
Korean	jeh-BAL
Russian	pah-ZHAH-lus-tah
Arabic	min FAD-lik
Hindi	krip-YA
Dutch	al-shuh-BLEEFT

TRAVEL TIP: "Please" is a universal sign of respect. Use it often when traveling.

THANK YOU!

LANGUAGE	PRONUNCIATION (ENGLISH)
English	**THANK yoo**
Spanish	**GRAH-see-ahs**
French	**mehr-SEE**
German	**DAHN-kuh**
Japanese	**ah-ree-gah-toh**
Mandarin Chinese	**shyeh-shyeh**
Italian	**GRAH-tsee-eh**
Portuguese	**oh-bree-GAH-do** (male) **oh-bree-GAH-dah** (female)
Korean	**gam-sah-ham-nee-dah**
Russian	**spa-SEE-bah**
Arabic	**SHOOK-ran**
Hindi	**dhun-yuh-VAAD**
Dutch	**DAHNK yuh**

TRAVEL TIP: A heartfelt "Thank you" in the local language goes a long way!

CHEERS!

LANGUAGE	PRONUNCIATION (ENGLISH)
English	CHEERZ
Spanish	sah-LOOD
French	sahn-TAY
German	PROHST
Japanese	kahn-PIE
Mandarin Chinese	gahn-BAY
Italian	sah-LOO-teh
Portuguese	sah-OO-jee
Korean	gun-BAY
Russian	zah zda-ROV-ye
Arabic	fee SIH-ha-tak
Hindi	CHEERZ
Dutch	PROHST

TRAVEL TIP: Make eye contact when you say "cheers." In many cultures it's a sign of respect and good luck.

BATHROOM

LANGUAGE	PRONUNCIATION (ENGLISH)
English	BATH-room
Spanish	BAHN-yo
French	twah-LET
German	toy-LET-uh
Japanese	toy-reh
Mandarin Chinese	shee-show jyen
Italian	BAHN-yo
Portuguese	bahn-YAIR-oh
Korean	hwa-JAHNG-shil
Russian	too-ah-LYET
Arabic	hah-MAHM
Hindi	BATH-room
Dutch	twah-LET

TRAVEL TIP: When in doubt, asking for the "toilet" or "restroom" is usually understood almost everywhere.

CAMPING TRIPS

Location: ______________________________

Date: ______________________________

Memories to Keep: ______________________________

____

____

Location: ______________________________

Date: ______________________________

Memories to Keep: ______________________________

____

____

Location: ______________________________

Date: ______________________________

Memories to Keep: ______________________________

____

____

Location: ______________________________

Date: ______________________________

Memories to Keep: ______________________________

____

____

ADVENTURE ARCHIVE

Sometimes the "bad" experiences are the most fun to look back on.

Location: ______

Date: ______

Memories to Keep: ______

Location: ______

Date: ______

Memories to Keep: ______

Location: ______

Date: ______

Memories to Keep: ______

Location: ______

Date: ______

Memories to Keep: ______

CRUISES TAKEN

Ship Name: ______________________________

Sail Date: ______________________________

Memories to Keep: ______________________________

____

____

Ship Name: ______________________________

Sail Date: ______________________________

Memories to Keep: ______________________________

____

____

Ship Name: ______________________________

Sail Date: ______________________________

Memories to Keep: ______________________________

____

____

Ship Name: ______________________________

Sail Date: ______________________________

Memories to Keep: ______________________________

____

____

ADVENTURE ARCHIVE

Don't forget to include who you were with & what you were celebrating.

Ship Name: ____________________

Sail Date: ____________________

Memories to Keep: ____________________

Ship Name: ____________________

Sail Date: ____________________

Memories to Keep: ____________________

Ship Name: ____________________

Sail Date: ____________________

Memories to Keep: ____________________

Ship Name: ____________________

Sail Date: ____________________

Memories to Keep: ____________________

OTHER ADVENTURES

Trip: ______________________________

Date: ______________________________

Memories to Keep: ______________________________

____

____

Trip: ______________________________

Date: ______________________________

Memories to Keep: ______________________________

____

____

Trip: ______________________________

Date: ______________________________

Memories to Keep: ______________________________

____

____

Trip: ______________________________

Date: ______________________________

Memories to Keep: ______________________________

____

____

ADVENTURE ARCHIVE

"Take care of all your memories. For you cannot relive them." – Bob Dylan

Trip: ______________________________

Date: ______________________________

Memories to Keep: ______________________________

____

____

Trip: ______________________________

Date: ______________________________

Memories to Keep: ______________________________

____

____

Trip: ______________________________

Date: ______________________________

Memories to Keep: ______________________________

____

____

Trip: ______________________________

Date: ______________________________

Memories to Keep: ______________________________

____

____

THE JOURNEY STAYS WITH YOU.

There will be places you remember for their
beauty, and others for how they changed you.

You'll collect moments you never planned for:
a turn down the wrong street,
a conversation that lingers,
a quiet second that somehow says everything.

Over time, the details may soften,
but the feeling stays.

So go—curious, open, and a little bit undone.
Take less than you think you need.
Notice more than you expect.
And trust that wherever you land,
you'll leave with something you didn't know
you were looking for.

Keep exploring.